The Gravedigger's Roots

Robert S. King

FutureCycle Press

Mineral Bluff, Georgia

SECOND EDITION
Copyright © 2009, 2012 Robert S. King
All Rights Reserved

Published by FutureCycle Press
Mineral Bluff, Georgia, USA

ISBN 978-0-9839985-6-3

for Diane,
an old soul and friend to mine

Contents

Life IV.
Dreams and Nightmares
39

Life V.
Divine Ale
45

Life VI.
Nightmares
53

Life VII.
Black Holes
59

Life VIII.
Nightmares
71

Life IX.
Progress
79

Life I.

In the Beginning Never Ends

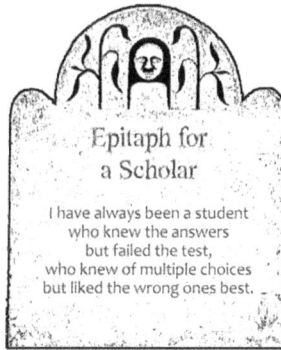

Epitaph for
a Scholar

I have always been a student
who knew the answers
but failed the test,
who knew of multiple choices
but liked the wrong ones best.

The Gravedigger Pacing His Cage

Because I have buried your fathers
you think the shovelman
looks death in the eye,
therefore is part of the murder.

I tell you I seldom see the eyes of the dead.
They are latched tight by the time
the corpses roll up to my feet.
Their lids are slammed by the anger
of failing to live forever.
Or they have simply grown weary of
opening and opening empty doors.

I tell you I am only here to close the lids,
to let their last breaths fall gently from our arms
like leaves in a cage full of dying wind.

Old friends, we are all changing colors
and falling off.

The Gravedigger's Black Apple Beating

I am told the seeds that spill
from a black apple
grow up again.
I am told the seeds that ooze
from a black heart
put down roots.

Not to rising sky they anchor,
and what is the value of dirt?
It has no wings unless I fling it.

My shovel is the heavy wing
flying too close to the earth.
Hawks hear it at the end of their dives,
the choking sound it makes
as it pierces the ground.

I am told, I tell myself . . .
Oh, I must fill my ears with one sound:
thin roots popping as the blade moves through.

A Matter of Time

I have wondered if the soul
comes back to listen to the acid hiss
in the melting of flesh,

this body, a hot whisper beneath
my digging, between melting plastic flowers
where I do my unsuccessful surgery on the earth,
my shadow moving like the hand of a clock,
trying not to think of the broiled weight
whose value I must lower into death,
somehow holding up my own,
in the quivering shadows, watching the sun
take the steam out of both of us.

Burying a Mute

Like a heavy tongue I lift my shovel
where a bee swills sugar
from a flower in the dung.
I hear the chest of the dead sigh
when I drop this weight,

for even from rotting flesh
needles of sweet scents rise up
like something one had forgotten to say.

Why the Dead Are so Passive

We honor the dead
by flinging dirt in their faces,
by planting thorny flowers
in their chests.
Like shepherds, we round them
up for cosmetic shearing.

They turn the other cheek
when we slap them,
as if to wake them,
as if to make them sting
for leaving us to the wars
of our mirrors.

We do not understand
what is eating them.

If God Pretends

God, pretend my soul is not a gypsy.
Pretend that ghosts do not cast shadows
that blacken the road in front of another man.
Do not pretend I am the wind that keeps coming back,
yet is forever blowing itself away,
and returning again with fouler breath,
or sweeping the body into a mouth of earth,
an earth that always spits up again,
that is full of bones and baby teeth
that cannot sever the nerves of the dead.

The Gravedigger Prays for Sunset

Let my shadow walk on hobbled feet,
cramped in shoes too small for the journey back,
turn its toes up near the warm stone of a fire,
the old ghost of frost hissing up in steam,
a dissipating cloud of memory.
Let the stone be soft as an egg
crushed beneath the weight of forgetting.
Let its yellow yolk be
a sun sinking into the earth.

Life II.

Dreams and Nightmares

Epitaph for an Orphan

Butterflies bloom on a tombstone
with no one's name
as if to be the flowers
no one knew to bring.

Snowhaunt

The snow comes
and adds two feet to my digging.
I remember once, as I was
turning white and burrowing,
how I fell through a rotten box,
crashed into the open arms of bone.

The skeleton held my head to its chest
as if I were her child
crying home from a fight.
I had to break her arms to breathe,
rose above her, brushed
her cold white skin from my coat.

Still, a ghost shivers within me,
a memory watching
the snow fatten her again.

The Ghost Observes His Body

Rising above it,
it seemed no more
than a dying and tangled root,
something to tie me to earth,
something now lost and only
rubbing around and around
a tree, its face a wilting
lily revolving toward light,
its voice a whimper of flesh
rubbing off on the bark.

The Ghost in the Barn Light

The bright animal brings the dawn in,
the sun a yolk in his pail of water.
In its mirror the bent farmer washes his hands,
fist deep in his own image, the seeds
in his pockets ready for burial.

Halfway to his digging,
he passes through my open arms,
through the porous weight of my caring.
I want to warm my hands on his brow, sing,
"Do not crack your head to hatch the soul . . ."
But I am music too light to touch down.

I pass through so many walls
without touching.

Life III.

High Society

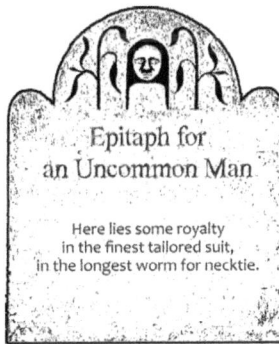

Epitaph for
an Uncommon Man

Here lies some royalty
in the finest tailored suit,
in the longest worm for necktie.

Blame It on Genealogy

Slowly the halo lowered
like a collar
around my neck,
then tightened its noose,
coiled till my face
grew red as an apple,
my eyes two black seeds,
squeezed around the core,
disappeared into the skin,
in my voice since
the whisper of a snake.

Discoveries of the Shovel

I cannot believe in silver spoons
when I was born with a shovel in my mouth.

Oh, I could say gravediggers think deeper than most,
say that the shovel is a tongue
which both uncovers and covers.

But a shovel turns the world
with a slurring voice,
like a man who cuts off his ears
and then gives his speech,
reading his own lips in a mirror.

It falls in my hands,
this metal tongue gone rusty,
and only when it hits a rock does it sing.

Yet the blade goes deeper than the man.
So I bend over like a question mark,
lean on it and feel it
sinking deeper than I care to go.

Say it should only nibble at the earth.
Say no to its rough handle, the finger
that pokes closest to my heart,
when it buries old splinters,
like little bodies,
in the gravedigger's hands.

The Gravedigger at the Costume Party

In the social gobble and cluck and crow
my silence is the dead center of attraction.
Though I come in my own dirty clothes,
they see me dressed as a worm,
see my black coat as a hole they might fall in.

Like a cold wind, I've come
in uninvited.
The King and Queen play host to shivers
where I shook their hands,
as if I'd held out my shovel to shake.
But these lovers dare not ask who I've held in my arms today,
whose skeletons I rattle like an honored guest,
shaking them with the hardest thing they'll ever learn.

Learn instead how Beauty and the Beast get up to dance,
how I twiddle my thumbs: two socialites going around
    in circles,
how as I ask for the honor
Beauty gets ugly.
Then I imagine myself the Right Reverend,
a preacher picking out the one worth saving,
the woman dressed like an open door,
imagine getting drunk and stinging
her prettiest cheek with my shovel,
she slamming in my face
the hard knob of her fist.

So I sit down in my place again,
my eye black as rotting fruit.
But who shall I tell next that finally
Death is no wallflower,
that, finally, I'll ask my shovel
to dance.

Condensation

The grave dirties all,
rich and poor in the same pocket,
the earth getting them mixed up.

In socialist wealth
they break new ground as flowers,
the royal and ragged hair
woven in a common web of dew,
their silver souls shining together through.

The Gravedigger's Workday

Not every moment is death.
Some seconds are firsts:
the chocolate-lip child giving
me advice on waking the dead,
a butterfly landing on my shovel,
decorating the deadliest day.

Sometimes firsts are second thoughts,
the child handing me a sweet,
the butterfly lifting
on a faint breath,
lifting with it a shadow
of rainbow, a streak
of quickening light only a child
or a soul can see.

Orphans Adopting Themselves

from our fathers
we inherit feet
from our mothers
long arms

we walk away
always reaching back

The Gravedigger's Closest Brother

The doctor does not ask me to dinner,
says I do not chew my food carefully,
that I gnaw all manners to the bone.
He says he is saving lives
while I toss them away,
says he scrubs before he operates,
while my muddy shovel infects the earth.

Doctor, a mutt such as I
never forgets where he buried his bones,
never forgets the afterglow of those bones.
They are family whose arms build bridges
to another shore, build ladders to climb from graves.
They feed those who remember them,
while you, suckled in the same litter,
abandon the starving stray
like someone you looked down on
and pronounced dead.

Moving to the City

Coming here,
broken farmers must believe
that the clouds plant their seeds in concrete
and skyscrapers grow:
tall stalks of corn,
long rows of one-way traffic,
horn honks replacing the songs of birds,
seeds spilling from their pockets fast as money.

Some return to a poor mule,
looking across a stubborn back
where the skyline is a monument:
the stalled traffic of tombstones.

The Gravedigger Wiping Sweat

The flesh is a tent I live in through the storm,
through which I sweat,
the skin leaking imperfect diamonds
that splatter at my feet,

till banks of flesh crumble into the red river,
finally to float in a fluid that keeps me from spoiling,
keeps me from lingering in the mourner's nose.
Then shall I be more glorious than a worm?
My only heir, it curls up in my sleep,
lies with me under the shovel still standing,
under the weathered etchings
where even raindrops
do not pause as they flow down through my name.

Doing the Dirty Work

Were I not the digger
I would be the corpse,
would be the dead wood,
a small town's witch to burn,
would be cut down like a tree left to rot
by the sharpest woodpeckers who want
to keep such black spots
from their fruits.

Were I not the dirty one,
umbrellas of canaries and crows
would drop upon me and dance
as if theirs were the beaks, the axes,
that whittled me down to size.
And when they lifted from me they would leave
black and white flowers on my face.

Enriched Soil

Both rich and poor are dirt poor in death,
but let me deposit whatever my worth
naked into a garden yet to be discovered.
If I must be dead and stripped of limbs,
let my old flesh be a seed that sprouts knowledge
that ages into grapes and probing vines.
Let the curious squeeze my fruit of good earth,
their mouths watering like treasure hunters,
as I grow larger and richer than I ever was,
until my bare bones stand up like trees
and leaf out for a lifetime.

Life IV.

Dreams and Nightmares

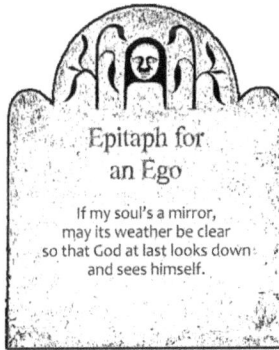

Epitaph for
an Ego

If my soul's a mirror,
may its weather be clear
so that God at last looks down
and sees himself.

The Gravedigger's Plot

Today a baptism of rain shines like a mirror,
helps me dig below the light,
helps me plot a seed of vengeance.
I lay this body on a hair-trigger spring,
tie a cold mirror to its chest,
tuck it in like a jack-in-the-box,
a joke on graverobbers.

When Jack pops from the earth,
who will look into his eyes?
Who will hear the word Surprise!
from his toothy grin?
Who will believe in the wild treasures
to which his petrified finger points?

Maybe they will get the point,
but maybe graverobbers just stare down
their mirrors, just pull his gold teeth,
laugh at the ancient joker
long after I've passed through the mirror.

Birthday Drive

With a yellowed map,
I'm lost and doing thirty
on cemetery roads that twitch like nerves.
And a dark poet is running beside me,
his face a mashed wad on my window,
waiting for me to shift lower, stop
and ask directions,
or waiting for the rubber ditches
to hold my fender down,
or waiting for me to do ninety
when he'll vault ahead, yawn
to swallow my headlights,
knowing in the dead end
my brakes will fail.

Little Mother of God

After church again on her favorite grave
the girl kneels and feeds mud pies to her doll.
Each Sunday she names him after the dead,
gives him the same birthday,
wipes the mud from his diaper.

She scolds him more than ten commandments,
gives him a teething ring shaped like a halo.
She says you forgot the Golden Rule
as she raises this ragged son
by the heels and spanks him,
needing to hear him cry,
needing to hear him say her name
and perform some miracle to save her.
She shakes and shakes him from sleep.
He is limp and does not answer prayers.
Then she says she is the mother of dead things.
She says she is spanking God.

Life V.

Divine Ale

Epitaph for
a Physician

Here lies a drunk surgeon
covered in the blood
of lives he saved,
who sliced a faint smile
on his own throat.

The Gravedigger Blows on the Bottle

While my shovel was tasting
ever deeper into a grave,
a drunk atheist swayed like a flagpole
and pissed into the grave through his shirttail,
saying he'd half a mind
to drink his body into the shape of a bottle.

Then he threw his bottle in the hole
and told me even the wind dies.

I say it moans awhile in the empty bottle
and moves on.

A Bottle to Float the Ocean

Once a mariner too old for the sea
sat on the ledge of a deepening grave,
watched his shadow getting drunk.
Before it passed out he told me

"I must be the first ever to shake
the hand of his own gravedigger,
but your hand is so cold,
it shivers my jitters. A stiff drink then
for a future stiff!"

He turned his bottle up like an hourglass;
his left hand seemed to wave goodbye
to ghosts from haunted beaches.
He tossed this near empty life
against the headstone,
a shattering, a christening for a new voyage.

"That's enough ale for a lifetime," he said
and put his ear to the grave,
a seashell where the wild waves
from distant shores took him under.

The Only Recognized Award for Drinking

If I polish my shovel,
its mirror reflects a cluster of stars.
I could stir them around with my finger
and believe myself closer to heaven.

But through the telescope of an empty bottle
I could believe that stars are made of spiked water,
that my shovel is the big dipper,
that I am drinking my way into paradise,
that I am staggering down its streets,
tickled by the feathers of angels,
celebrated, the first drunk of heaven.

The Gravedigger's Night Out

Tonight I'll get high
with the undertakers,
pass around the suds
to wash this dirt from my eyes,
stagger home under stars
and in a golden fall release
my drunk bladder, my brain
on a stone,
on a name etched into my sleep.

Morning foams into my mouth,
a memory,
and I am out of the mind's soap.

Let my tongue be a bar of lye soap
for a shovelman who bathes in memory
scrubs with dirt.
Let my brain be a sponge
I wring out every morning
when shadows steam up in the sun.
Let me pour whiskey on the sponge
and stand near the fire,
rubbing my fingers together
till they smoke and spark.

The Old Deeds of the Gravedigger

What wine has aged enough for heaven?
What will get the angels drunk
so they wrap their wings around me
and take me this time?
When is the morning they wake me
with a musical kiss?

I wake only to the sting of a cold shovel at my cheek,
know I will rise like a mortgaged farmer
to plant dead seed in the field,
know that the black cat
will ambush my back again,
that I will look behind me
to see what has been torn off,
even recall being slapped into life,
crying for the nipple that makes me drunk,
writing another of my names in the dirt
where winds smack of rain on a night
when I can't wean myself from the bottle.

Then give me the night in a bottle!
Let me get drunk on a good memory.
Let me stagger through colliding
streets of Pompeii,
buying land dirt cheap in the rumble,
in my arms stacking deeds up to the chin.

But I own not even the dirt
I spray under my shoulder
and only the cold lips of the shovel
kiss me back.

Life VI.

Nightmares

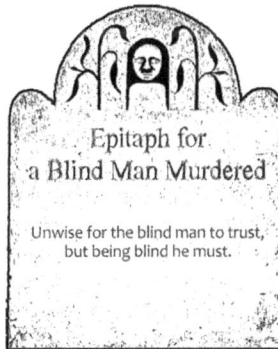

Epitaph for
a Blind Man Murdered

Unwise for the blind man to trust,
but being blind he must.

The Black Lady

Old owl pumps up the night.
I come looking for my shovel,
but come instead into the light
of the lady.
I squint toward her,
following the moths, the boneglow
of small fossils. Beside the lady
stands my shovel on a mound of dirt.

Owl pumps and pumps.
I answer, blowing on my bottle of rum.
The lady conducts the winds:
four flutes silken,
lift and strum my hair,
weave me into her arms
and her song.

Owl perches on the stone.
The lady slides me down into its shadow,
our fingers scratching another name
on that ugly tooth
that juts from the gums of earth.

The Death of Magic

The ugliest of three sisters,
who once kept her silk face smooth,
willed me her wand.
I am told its hollow spine
was full of stars
once caught in her eyes.
I broke its back on a stone;
its stars crawled off
to weave their webs.

Another Sunday Storm

An exorcist sweating out his soul,
I lie awake listening to the liquid meanings
of rain roar through my gutters,
blow wet kisses to my windows.

Each drop seems a brother, or myself,
whose fall I failed to break;
seems a sister, or myself,
whose tears salted the wounds.
Yet each I've let down
would kiss me still,

I who seem but an empty lifeboat
washed up on their shores.

Life VII.

Black Holes

Epitaph for
a Ghost

Now I'm less solid than wind.
I drive my fingers
through this pine box
without leaving holes.
A ghost is himself a hole.

The Suit with the Missing Buttons

On a door nail
my black suit hangs by the neck,
its pockets swollen with moths,
their brief wings turned to flakes of ash.

Moths eat little of the fabric of darkness.
Only they chew small holes
where the stars fall through.

Outside the late sun, a little wheel,
bounces on the horizon.
The darkness of my suit spreads over the bed.
One more button lets go,
rolls around the floor,
its voice disappearing
into a silent hole.

Karma of a Gravedigger

I am told, I am told to toss
the dirt over my shoulder,
let the back be stiff, grind
and shift with gates and graveyard hinges,
let the black sweat mingle with dew
and gypsy mist that rises from
the husk I am planting.

I am told not to let my work pile up,
to work faster than the falling leaves
which fill the holes and rattle against
the tombstones like a million old bones.

I am told not to speak of
fresh dirt bubbling in the rain,
only to say how it clings to my cuffs—
not how it erodes my hours,
how the sky if it had a nose
would blow it on my sanity,
how the blue veins flex on my arms
like roads I have yet to cover.

Who will cover me?
Who will dig into the black heart but me
when I alone know the shovel's song?
Who, when I have refused a life of lips,
will kiss my forehead in the coffin?

What physician will pinch my nostrils
and breathe his chemicals into my lungs,
so my chest may rise like a sigh?

I am told the blood goes in circles,
that it washes back something you had thrown away.

So let this blood turn clear as sweat,
cool as dewdrops, perfect as diamonds
that sink into the earth and never rise again.

But if I must come back far-sighted as a mole,
and they lift me squinting by the heels,
let me not cry no matter how hard they slap.
For the arms that have held me close
have always been the weakest vines
where I have grown little, snapped off, and withered,
to become the oldest soul at judgment day,
the oldest one turned away.

Again and again I am told I am
the spirit's bastard,
with half a dirty face,
too ugly for heaven,
too beautiful for hell.

The Gratitude of the Dead

Some murdered men rest in pieces.
I am he who rakes this puzzle of flesh into one pile,
trying to fathom the loose fit of violence,
feeling a million cavernous mouths
relieve history of its debts.

What is eating us is seldom bright or beautiful.
So I say the bowels of earth should be full of light,
that I should bury this dead one with glow worms,
their light dripping down from my shovel,
curling up into little halos
around his brilliant peace.

He might even thank me
were his tongue not tied with worms.

Darkness Too Is a Mirror

Nothing taunts me like the moon
which sits atop a tombstone
and mimics all the faces I've covered up.

Who sends it here
night after night, life after life?
It comes to swell full of generosity
and shed some light.
Or to make each marble slab a mirror,
though I have travelled so many mirrors
and come back alone,
have learned to mole my way
in the absence of light.

Yet there's no dirt black enough,
no soil thicker than memory,
to douse the flames of those I've lost,
as the oldest stars come out like moths
swarming about this moon,
seekers fleeing darkness as if it buried truth,
while I and my shovel go sinking so deep
and so coldly into night.

The Gravedigger's Sunshades

They don't know I watch them
count their cash from a safe distance,
how they admire their manicures, pick their noses,
scratch themselves in private places.

They only know how warm is park bench,
how warm the granite markers in sunlight,
how tightly children hug,
what plenty they'll spend on good taste today.

They don't know that I see their shadows
growing shorter and deeper, etching themselves
into names wearing down with time.
They don't know that my shadow
is mixing with theirs
and makes nothing better.

I only know that someday is cold in the shade,
poor company on that day when
even the great grandchildren
are shadows none can name.

The Gravedigger's Shade Tree

Like this windy oak tree,
I cannot leave this place.
The best I can do is dig deeper,
tangled in my own roots.

I can only lean,
wave my limbs at those
who seem to know the way,
who seem lighter than wind,

while I bend over backwards
to the breaking point.

The Gravedigger's Legacy

I am told to keep my shadow busy.
I am to some the one to do a lowly job,
and because years have bent me
lowest to the earth,
I do it well into the fading light.

As the night shifts, my shadow works
within me like a chill,
yet I know while I feel his shivers
that I have time to burn.

The other side of the moon turns around tonight,
shades my face from the stars
climbing higher above me,
while I dig for an answer come from darkness.
My shovel frames a perfect black window.
I keep my head just above it,
watch the lost world of foggy street lights
swaying and smearing,
a thick wind turning visible and mean,
wrecking bats and rescues.

Time is another impatient hole
I cannot crawl out of.
I have never gotten to the bottom of a grave,
nor have I seen who in the black hole
twists the brightest light into nothing.

And I dare not weep
for those more dead than I.
Tears could harden into glass,
cut my outstretched hands
that could not break their fall.

The Graveyard Shift

I prefer the dead of night,
but hold back its chill for a living
while moths pop against the lantern.

How deceiving is light
that holds out its arms
only to blind and burn,
while this cold shovel and this dark hole
offer nothing but the whole truth.

Shift over, I snuff out the lamp,
squint at a million moth holes
in the moonless sky.

Around me the godless moths swim
in a nightmare of black blood,
splattering the glazed headstones,
the ghost of redemption oozing
along the etchings.

My nightmare is light
that shows me where I'm blind.
My sweet dream is oblivion
that keeps me in the dark.

Life VIII.

Nightmares

Epitaph for
a Corporate Lawyer

To steal from the blind is bad,
but is good practice.

Dream of the Hollow Bone

Going to war,
I met a shivering skeleton
who'd already been.

My skin was still clean
and squeaked in the wind.
But he strummed his ribs like a harp,
his skull a hollow drum in the rain.
Where his heart used to be was a mirror.

He said, "I am looking for the one
who tore my flesh off like old clothes,
the one who's made me so long wear nothing.
If I do not find him you will do."

As he opened his arms
long serpents of rain curled around them.

Suddenly my skin glassed clear as water,
poured into a puddle at my feet.
In the grave my bones spelled out his name,
as long snakes of rain whispered lullabies,
as black cloudbursts of buzzards fell,
and the muddy music of earth caved in.

Communion

Head bent over, a young man by candle light
ate from a plate full of ashes.
He smiled at me, an old man.
"You are going to say phoenix, aren't you?"
Teeth stealing light from the candle,
he lifted a warm, gray spoon:
"You see, old man, this is my father."

"Won't you join me," he said,
reaching to shake my hand.

Graveside Pyre

Through fog and smoke the polished tombstones stand,
like monuments or border guards of once great nations

or mirrored tips of icebergs,
where fire flirts with its own brief brilliance,
watching its flames tug lower, cooling down
from white, to blue, to red, to the yellow
jaundice of history.

And no stoker, no world-travelled wind,
no chemistry book fans back the flame.
The bodies it feeds on are torn away,
belched up in so much smoke,
cinders of brief torches pulsing down
into the dark ages between so many stars.

But a good fire dies slowly,
does not let the ice age come at once.
Even Eskimos know the world is only
cold in unattended places,
know some trailblazer with a thousand
new books of matches
will rub his own hands into friction,

to win the cold war,
to build his fire in a blanket of snow,
to burn another hole in the earth.

The Crow's Orbit

My youth and my old age
are spent in boxes.
Centuries of falling in
and climbing out of holes.
The whole of me together and lost,
one soul trying to keep
one pain at a time,
one loss at a time,
yet many scattered hopes all at once
sticking to the steady movement of decay.

And what has my flesh gained
but something to wash off,
different color dirts,
a variety of burial gowns,
a multitude of faces burrowing into chests
(and even some who smile at my departures).

And why of all the hopes I've built
is the tombstone the only thing named after me?

I ask, no I beg, over and over
inside a box and out,
how can I lift and throw away
this many heavy stones
whose cool marbles wink
in both sunlight and rain,

making my name hard to read
and even harder to remember?

In what life will I sit on a dozen eggs
without crushing one?
In what year do I resculpt these shells
and fly off into some answer
that goes beyond the nearest stars,
goes further into the black hole of truth,
there to be, and not becoming.

Yet I have always been a bird afraid of heights.
Years of limping around in different corpses,
not knowing in which grave
or which heaven I belong.
But none of them keeps me.
I pop, re-pop out of tombs and wombs,
a cuckoo clock, a senseless jack-in-the-box,
coming out with the stump of one black wing on my back,
coming out mad and crying,
spitting and spitting dirt
that a child by nature must learn to eat.

Yes, I come out with my mouth
still in the same shape of its last pain.
I cry for brighter mirrors,
but my lips round into a circle
and my words bellow forth
from the deepest holes I've known.

On every tombstone
is a crow,
a black braggart
who has flown through the dark ages,
found nothing else
to land on.

Life IX.

Progress

Epitaph for
a Gravedigger

Another womb, another tomb,
I'm always in the dark
of their waiting room.

Against the Graveyard's Greater Wall

Against it the wind piles up and dies.
It is star high, worm deep.
Hawks explode against it;
roots bleed against its sharp edges.
Leaves clatter halfway up a ladder,
then flutter down
into the dead eye of the storm.

All roads merge against it
and wrinkle up into dead ends,
all miles ever travelled,
all the old footprints
twisted into the same old story.

Only an inner rain almost turns it clear,
this great wall,
this mirror.

The Gravedigger's Pay Dirt

The wind starts early today,
scolds the grave, my lunch box, my shovel,
throws dirt back into a half-eaten hole to finish.

My lunch is left over from a previous life,
whose appetite was never satisfied,
whose bread turned hard to match its sleepless eyes.

I'm old and creaky, but regret is louder.
I have no teeth for the hard bread I've become,
have no bite except the hole my shovel makes.

Someday the grave will be a good place to hide.
Today I have no good place to put the dirt,
except on the chest of someone someone lost.
I hear a sigh when the weight is dropped.

It's always someone else's grave,
where respectfuls sway like trees about to fall.
Many of their tears fall inward,
but some splatter on the one they knew
and some land on familiar shoulders,
dark-coated trunks leaning on one another
as their leaves, like money, blow away.

Hunger—not heart, not greed—is life.
I feel empty but do not wish to eat
a legacy that would rot me from the inside

like the fruit of the dead curling black.
Still my heart stops for its lunch,
a thin-skinned bag bleeding through.

I must swallow what little life it gives,
put it to work, make a living
that gets paid every Deathday.
The black sweat of my brow hardens
in the wind that works late today.

Where the Wind Writes Our Names

Against the wind I think
of these tombstones as doors.
The dirt from my shovel
is whistling through a keyhole.

I feel the corpse of history going through,
ash and dirt piling up
darkness on the other side,
watch the names of so much flesh fly through,
see only the wind come back
in the same shape.

The Gravedigger's Roots

There is no telling how high above me
high winds cut into the mountain,
moan through the hollow trees,
split the well-rooted at golden rings,
forge them into coffin nails,
drive their splinters
down the heart of the gale.

The dead stick beneath my fingernails.
My trunk too is brittle and many ringed,
but I began at the bottom
and have worked my way down.

There is no telling how far I can go.

Why Graveyards Are Full of Bright Birds

At dusk I lock the gate
to keep the living out.
I am told the wind comes here to die.
It falls and a thousand wings
darken down,
nothing to hold them to the sky.

A Wingbeat of Hope

Suppose gravity suddenly floated off into space,
lifting for the first time
the corners of our mouths.
Suppose the sky a deep blue pool
and we the divers
in a broadcast of waves moving through.

Fancy rainbows are sliding boards
into some heaven that demands
no soul's ransom for its gold.

Imagine that all dark angels
put on the jewelry of stars,
that all black holes of graves
let rise their luminous ghosts,
that all things bright enough to blind
melt together into vision.

See then the lodestar,
magnet to our rusting bones.
Believe then that the anchors on our backs
begin to beat like wings.

Feeding the Body of Earth

if one of us who were cloven to bits
could remember the forest our body on our journey
if one of us could feel the forest sleeping
in us on our stone pillows
then we'd awake all of us by a road
with our murderers in our arms

and we'd rock them in our arms
but one by one we dead fly out of our senses
one by one the tongue the nose the fingers the ears
would all of us forgive the battle for being long
and though our mortal wits fall in five separate fields
five decomposing memories
the wind is still a nerve between us
a spirit clearer than blood
that moves through the grass
to soothe amputated eyes
looking back at us between the blades

and their gaze might hold forever the last thing they saw:
the limbs lift an ax and hack the trunks down
or see each man a battlefield reclaimed by weeds

but there would swell an oak from every weed
there would shine new eyes in every nest
and one of us would be all of us

all our pieces in a gown of acid
one by one dissolving into the body of earth
one by one into the hues of its wings
and one by one of us the crows would drop bits of us
    to their young
and all the roads our nerves would twitch and open wide

Acknowledgments

Grateful acknowledgments are made to the following publications in which these poems first appeared, sometimes in earlier versions:

Black Bear Review: "Condensation," "Graveside Pyre," "Moving to the City"
California Quarterly: "Discoveries of the Shovel," "The Gravedigger Blows on the Bottle"
The Chariton Review: "Feeding the Body of Earth"
The Cape Rock: "A Matter of Time"
Dead Angel: "Why Graveyards Are Full of Bright Birds"
Great River Review: "Blame It on Genealogy"
Hampden-Sydney Poetry Review: "Darkness Too Is a Mirror," "The Gravedigger Wiping Sweat"
Hellas: "Epitaph for a Blind Man Murdered"
Immortelles: Poems About Life and Death by New Southern Poets (Xavier Review Press): "The Gravedigger's Night Out"
The Kenyon Review: "If God Pretends," "A Wingbeatof Hope"
Loch Raven Review: "The Gravedigger's Pay Dirt," "Graveyard Shift," "The Gravedigger's Plot"
Lungfish Review: "Why the Dead Are so Passive"
Pendragon: "The Ghost in the Barn Light," "The Ghost Observes His Body"
The Plastic Tower: "The Gravedigger Pacing His Cage"
Poem: "The Black Lady," "Burying a Mute," "The Death of Magic," "Karma of a Gravedigger," "The Old Deeds

of the Gravedigger," "The Gravedigger Prays for Sunset,"
"Snowhaunt"
Poems That Thump in the Dark: "The Suit with the Missing
Buttons"
Poetic Space: "Where the Wind Writes Our Names"
Riverrun: "Dream of the Hollow Bone," "The Gratitude of the
Dead," "The Gravedigger's Black Apple Beating"
Slant: "Birthday Drive"
Soundings East: "The Only Recognized Award for Drinking"
Underground Voices: "The Gravedigger's Workday,"
"The Crow's Orbit"
Visions International: "Against the Graveyard's Greater Wall"
Whistling Shade: "The Gravedigger's Legacy"
Windless Orchard: "Orphans Adopting Themselves"
Xanadu: "Communion"
Zuzu's Petals: "Doing the Dirty Work"

The author extends special thanks to Shared Roads Press, now
defunct, for publishing the first edition of *The Gravedigger's
Roots* and giving FutureCycle Press the rights to the second
edition.

*Cover/book design and author photo by Diane Kistner,
dkistner@futurecycle.org; photo of spade in a heap of soil
by Pidjoe; epitaph art adapted from the Luther Trowbridge
headstone; book type, Deja Vu Sans Condensed with
Euphorigenic titling*

About FutureCycle Press

FutureCycle Press is dedicated to publishing lasting English-language poetry and flash fiction books, chapbooks, and anthologies in both print-on-demand and ebook formats. Founded in 2007 by long-time independent editor/publishers and partners Diane Kistner and Robert S. King, the press incorporated as a nonprofit in 2012. A number of our editors are distinguished poets and authors in their own right, and we have been actively involved in the small press movement going back to the early seventies.

Our annual anthology, *FutureCycle*, combines poetry and flash fiction. The FutureCycle Poetry Book Prize and honorarium is awarded annually for the best full-length volume of poetry we publish in a calendar year. We are dedicated to giving all authors we publish the care their work deserves, making our catalog of titles the most distinguished it can be, and paying forward any earnings to fund more great books.

We've learned a few things about independent publishing over the years. We've also evolved a unique, resilient publishing model that allows us to focus mainly on vetting and preserving for posterity the most books of exceptional quality without becoming overwhelmed with bookkeeping and mailing, fundraising activities, or taxing editorial and production "bubbles." To find out more about what we are doing, come see us at www.futurecycle.org.